DAN
THE PIONEER OF ISRAEL

With an Appendix:

WHY DAN WAS NOT SEALED AMONG THE 144,000
(REV. VII)

BY

COLONEL J. C. GAWLER
Keeper of the Crown Jewels

A REPRINT FROM AN EDITION PUBLISHED
BY
**W. H. GUEST, 20 WARWICK LANE,
PATERNOSTER ROW
LONDON
1880**

PUBLISHED BY

ARTISAN PUBLISHERS
P.O. Box 1529
Muskogee, OK 74402
Phone (918) 682-8341

Copyright ©1984
by Artisan Publishers

PREFACE

In the following chapters I have traced but a mere outline. To have brought forward all the evidence that might be adduced would have occupied volumes. I trust there is sufficient in these pages to induce others to study them themselves; but of one thing I feel assured, *The British Empire stands or falls with the Anglo-Israel theory*, because:

1. From a *strategical* point of view, in the approaching crisis (on the dissolution of Turkish Empire), which may take place within a year or two, but may extend over the next twenty years, *the Power that gains Syria will control the British Empire.*

2. From a *Scriptural* point of view, if we, *not being Israel*, lay hold on Syria, we shall be very soon cleared out of it again. Compare also Jer. 30:11.

This question, which statesmen have dreaded, is called "The Eastern Question," but in Bible language "The controversy of Zion" (Isa. 34:8), or, *who is to succeed to the country promised by God to Abraham?* (Isa. 63:4).

J. C. Gawler

Tower of London, Dec., 1879.

CONTENTS

CHAPTER I

CHAPTER II
DANAI OF GREECE ARE DANNITES OF ISRAEL

CHAPTER III
DAN IN THE BLACK SEA

CHAPTER IV
DAN AMONG THE SCYTHIANS

CHAPTER V

DANNANS, OR DANES, OF SCANDINAVIA, IRELAND, AND SCOTLAND

APPENDIX

DAN, THE PIONEER OF ISRAEL

CHAPTER I

Dan, the name–History of Dan gathered from the Bible–Intimacy with the Phoenicians–Israelitish and Phoenician enterprise–Prefix Don, or Dan.

The Tribe of Dan by its enterprise and vigour has made itself one of the most conspicuous branches of Jacob's family. Its ancestor was the son of one of the concubines, and was the firstborn of Rachel's household. *"God hath judged me,"* said Rachel, and she called his name *"Dan,"* which means to *judge*, to *rule*. This word, while perhaps on that occasion first started as a surname, has been perpetuated as a title in the Gothic, Anglo-Saxon, and English. In these languages Din, Dun, Don, and Dan, signify *ruler, master*. The expression is repeatedly used by Shakespeare, Spenser, Chaucer, Prior, and others. The Spanish, too, from close contact for ages with the Hebrew, have engrafted it in their title of Don. It is in use in our universities to designate a professor or university official.*

---

*At a conference in Bayswater, in 1875, one of the opposition speakers took exception to these remarks. He believed that the university and Spanish *Don* was derived from the Latin Dominus; and, as for *Dun*, in Scotch it meant a *hill*. I had not an opportunity of replying, but the objector seemed not to know how thoroughly he was confirming what had been asserted. He did not seem to reflect that Rome, who was not even an infant in arms when Rachel said, *"God hath judged me,"* must have coined her *Dominus* and *damno* from the Hebrew or Phoenician. And, as regards Dun; Don, likewise, in the

Gothic, means *hill* as well as *master*, and in this double signification they merely resemble the word *eminence*, which in Ireland especially is used as a title. *Dun* and *Don* therefore being identical, how come they to mean a *hill*, and yet often to be the name of a *river*, unless it be for the same reason that another form of the name was once also imposed on a *town*–viz., *"After the name of Dan their father."* (Judges 18:29)

———————

How often do we see in the Bible that the name of an individual foreshadows the character and career. Dan's name given by Rachel implies authority and vigour, and Jacob, when bestowing his blessings (Gen. 49:16), repeats and confirms it. *"Dan shall judge his people,"* said the venerable patriarch, and proceeded to name other characteristics implying great wisdom and astuteness. The serpent is the Scripture symbol of wisdom. (Gen. 3:1; Matt. 10:16) In dealing with foes his plans would be laid with wisdom and secrecy, and his action would be unlooked for and rapid.

"I have waited for Thy salvation, O Lord," is the ejaculation of Jacob as he concluded his blessing to Dan. What was in the patriarch's mind? Did a vision of Dan's future career pass in review before him? Did he see the pioneers of Israel by land and sea carrying on their enterprise and explorations, trading among the Grecian Islands into the Black Sea, up the various rivers, crossing Asia Minor, exploring Europe, scouring the Mediterranean, on into the broad Atlantic, meeting the overland parties at the Baltic, settling in Denmark, and making a secret secure little hiding-place and sanctuary for centuries in Ireland, and other settlements in England and Scotland? And did the patriarch still see this Tribe in the van leading back to the Land of Promise to take up their first place, the most Northerly, in the day when the Lord shall beat off *"from the channel of the river of Egypt"*? in that day when the Lord shall *"bind up the breach of His people, and heal the stroke of their wound."*

Shortly after the Israelites left Egypt, the Tribe of Dan numbered of fighting men alone, *"from twenty years old and upwards all that were able to go forth to war, 62,700"* (Num. 1:38, 39); and their very lot that fell to them in the Promised Land was calculated to stir up the inherent spirit. Their lot was on the coast from Ashkelon to Joppa, and it was in the purposes of God *"too little for them"* (Josh. 19:40-47), B.C. 1443. So in a very few years (Judges 18), 600 of them with their families and baggage marched off northward to the spurs of Hermon and conquered a corner of Bashan. With a sort of *esprit de corps* and veneration for their ancestor, which marked the whole career of this Tribe, they called the name of their new conquest *"Dan, after the name of Dan their father."* (ver. 29) It bears the impress of their determination to assert themselves, and to verify their name to *rule* and be *masters*.

Much was probably done in the following years, but the Scriptures were written with one object, and hence, matter irrelevant to that object finds no place. Yet it came within the purpose of God to tell us that about B.C. 1285 (Judges 5:17) Dan had ships and got on board them when an invasion threatened; and, as for many years previous to this, Israel had been for long intervals under the yoke of Jabin, King of Canaan, of the King of Moab, the King of Mesopotamia, and of the Philistines. Dan must have been paying some attention to nautical matters, and the love of enterprise and freedom had probably considerably reduced the numbers left behind, who, unable then to cope with their enemies, finally thought it more prudent to follow. Certain it is that the Tribe of Dan entirely disappeared from Palestine. In I Chron. 4-6, which were written after the Babylonish captivity, Dan, as well as Zebulun and Asher, also coast Tribes, are omitted from the genealogies. Alford, on Rev. 7, quotes several writers as believing that Dan became *"as good as extinct."* Grotius quotes a Jewish tradition that this Tribe was early reduced to one family, named Huss, which is known to have perished in the wars before the time of Ezra. Eldad, a Jewish writer in the 14th or 9th century, writing to the Spanish Jews, saying that "in Jeroboam's time (B.C. 975) the Tribe of Dan, being unwilling to shed their brethren's blood, took a resolution of leaving their country."*

*Sailman. *Researches in the East*, 1818.

Whatever became of them, therefore, they disappeared from Palestine entirely. But, that it was not an *extinction*, we know from the fact that it is recorded in Ezek. 48, that in the final division of the land, which has not yet taken place, Dan comes in for his share at the head of the list.

The Old Testament, having put us in this position, gives us one clue where to look for the lost, and then leaves it. The New Testament, to my mind, furnishes another clue as to their whereabouts at a later period, by omitting the Tribe altogether from the sealing of the 144,000. (Rev. 7)

The Old Testament clue is as follows: Ezekiel (27:17-19), writing circ. B.C. 588 against Tyre and pronouncing her doom, says, *"Judah and the land of Israel"* (not the Israelites themselves *who were then in captivity*, but such inhabitants as there were) *"were thy merchants. .... Dan also and Javan going to and fro occupied in thy fairs."* Now in three places in Daniel, where Alexander the Great is distinctly indicated, and one in Zechariah, Javan is translated *"Greece";* Josephus also (i. Vi. 1) mentions Javan as being *Greece.* Hence Dan is indicated as in company with Greece trading with Tyre.

The Danites and men of Tyre were naturally on very intimate terms. It was a very remarkable privilege to be accorded to a foreign nation – if foreign – to be allowed to help in building Solomon's Temple. The Danites and people of Tyre intermarried; the cunning craftsman especially sent by Hiram to superintend the work of the Temple was the son of a man of Tyre, and his mother was of the daughters of Dan. (II Chron. 2:14)

Now it is necessary to bear in mind this intimate connection recorded in the Bible of the Phoenicians with Israel, especially with Dan. We must remember the numerical strength of this Tribe alone, 62,700 fighting men (*i.e.,* neither old men nor boys), shortly after their leaving Egypt. (Num. 2:25,26) We must consider the schooling they had had with the then most advanced nation in the world in literature and science. Moses *"was learned in all the wisdom of the Egyptians"* (Acts 7:22); and, beyond all this, we must remember God's promises concerning Israel. The seed of Abraham, Isaac, and Jacob would not be likely to collapse and wither when in contact with other races! We must bear all this in mind because we find Grecian, Irish, Scandinavian, and English histories teeming

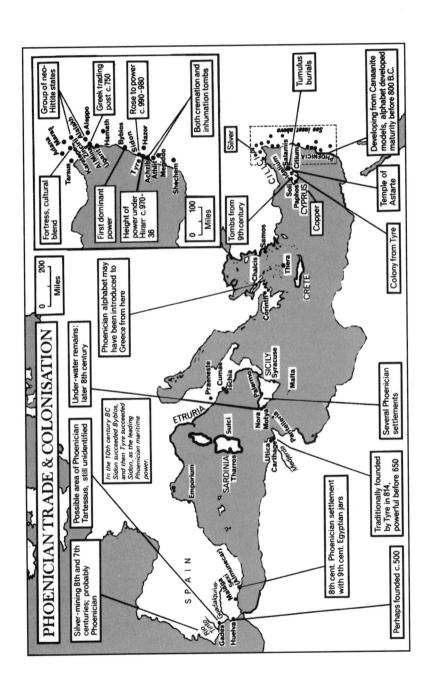

PHOENICIAN TRADE & COLONISATION

Silver-mining 8th and 7th centuries; probably Phoenician

Possible area of Phoenician Tartessus, still unidentified

Under-water remains: later 8th century

Phoenician alphabet may have been introduced to Greece from here

In the 10th century BC Sidon succeeded Byblos, and then Tyre succeeded Sidon, as the leading Phoenician maritime power.

Perhaps founded c.500

8th cent. Phoenician settlement with 9th cent. Egyptian jars

Traditionally founded by Tyre in 814, powerful before 650

Several Phoenician settlements

Colony from Tyre

Group of neo-Hittite states

Greek trading post c.750

Rose to power c. 990–980

Both cremation and inhumation tombs

Tumulus burials

Silver

Developing from Canaanite models, alphabet developed maturity before 800 B.C.

Fortress, cultural blend

First dominant power

Height of power under Hiram c. 970–36

Temple of Astarte

Tombs from 9th century

Copper

0   100
Miles

0   200
Miles

Map labels:

Adana, Masat, Tarsus, Karatepe, Alalakh, Aleppo, Al Mina, Athira, Ugarit, Hamath, Byblos, Sidon, Tyre, Achzib, Hazor, Athlit, Megiddo, Shechem

CILICIA, Soli, Salamis, Citium, Paphos, CYPRUS, PHOENICIA

See inset above

SPAIN, Río Tinto, Gades, Guadalquivir, Málaga, Sexi (Almuñecar), Huelva

Emporium, SARDINIA, Tharros, Sulci, Nora, Motya, ETRURIA, Panormus, Utica, Carthage, Mediterranean, Praeneste, Cumae, Ischia, Palermo, SICILY, Syracuse, Malta

Samos, Chalcis, Corinth, Thera, CRETE

-5-

with notices of a certain race called Danai, or Dannans, or Dannonii, who are either called Phoenicians, or mentioned in company with Phoenicians. Almost wherever Phoenicians are said to have traded, there we either hear of these Danai, or we find a river or district stamped with the name of Dan according to the early custom recorded of that Tribe in the Scriptures.

In a lecture delivered to Jewish working men and their families at the Jews' Infant School on May 23rd, 1875, the Rev. A. L. Green stated as follows (*Jewish Chronicle*, May 28th, 1875):

> "Our forefathers in their happiest times, in the golden age of the nation's glory, were indeed the public carriers of their day, travellers for commercial enterprise to all the then known countries near and far. The ships of Solomon rivalled the Phoenician navy. The Ports of Elath and Sziongeber were filled with the ships of Tarshish, which sailed down the AElanitic Gulf of the Red Sea on to the Indian Ocean, to Ophir, to Sheba, to Arabia Felix, to India and Ceylon, and through the Pillars of Hercules; brought home copper from Cyprus and tin from Spain, possibly from Cornwall. The Talmud is filled with special regulations bearing on the exceptional wants springing from these various avocations. Synagogues were from earliest times attached to special centres of industry and frequented by special traders, and a workman's ritual was specially arranged to suit the artisan, the landsman, and the seafarer. The pursuits of commerce, in its various ramifications, were covered by an admirable code of international law. The laws of agency and insurance and hypothecation were codified. Promissory notes and bills of exchange were formulated even in Mishnaic times."

We may here pause to ask, What has become of this spirit of enterprise and love of adventure, this active, roving, restless spirit? It surely does not exist in the Jews of the present day. What has become of the commercial sailor race which this learned Jewish lecturer describes when speaking of Israel *"in the golden age of the nation's glory"?* It assuredly does not describe the

Jews of the present day, but all must admit that it is an admirable description of ourselves!

In the *Manual of Ancient History* (p. 214) I read as follows:

> "From the middle of the sixteenth to the middle of the fourteenth century B.C., several colonies from Egypt, Phoenicia, and Phrygia settled in different parts of Greece, bringing with them the improvements in the arts and sciences that had been made in their respective countries. A Phoenician colony under Cadmus settled in Boeotia; he was the first who introduced the use of letters into Greece. . . . . The Phoenicians were at that period the *undisputed masters* of the Aegean." p. 86 – "Cyprus was not only a colony, but a province of the Tyrians. . . . . From Cyprus they extended their settlements to Crete, thence they proceeded to Africa, Sicily, and Sardinia. . . . . The Spanish peninsula – called in Scripture Tarshish – was the country with which the Tyrians had the most lucrative trade; and the colonies they established soon became independent States. Colonies were also planted beyond the Straits of Gibraltar. Trade was extended to the British Islands and to the coasts of the North Sea. It is known that the Phoenicians preceded the Greeks in forming commercial establishments along the coasts of Asia Minor and the shores of the Black Sea. . . . . In the Eastern seas they had establishments on the Persian and Arabian Gulfs."

Now let us track Dan's footprints by this Phoenician light, and we shall find that almost wherever the Phoenicians have been, there, or in close proximity, on the name of some place, river, or province, the name of Dan is imprinted, as they did in their earliest independent conquest in Palestine. We have, then, on the Red Sea, *Don-gola;** in Greece, *Caly-don*, a river of Attica (*Strabo*), the Eri-*dan*; Make-*don*; the *Dan*ube, *Dan*astris (now Dniester), Danapris (now Dnieper), and the *Don*.

---

*The substance of this paper was delivered as a lecture at Clapham in 1876, when the Rev. Canon Titcomb, now Bishop of Rangoon, very kindly took the chair. Although a staunch Anglo-Israelite and a believer in Dan as an enterprising pioneer, he took exception to my claiming *Don*-gola as having anything to do with Dan, and thought it was "making Dan ubiquitous" to trace him to Africa. But, in point of fact, it is one of the easiest to defend, for in Dongola and the neighbourhood are at this moment two bodies of people – the Falashas and Karmantas – professing the Jewish faith, calling themselves Israelites, and acknowledged by our English Jews.

Before speaking of the people in Greece, and of the Colchians in the eastern corner of the Black Sea, we will take the probable route of an exploring overland party up the Danube to its source in the mountains of Switzerland, and there pick up another river, the Rho-*dan* (now the Rhone), down to the sea at the ancient so-called Phoenician town of Massilia, now Marseilles, and thence across to Sar-*din*-ia. Back again into Switzerland we pick up the Eri-dan (now the Po), flowing eastward through Venetia to the Adriatic. While in Venetia I would call your attention to the following: We may infer from Ezek. 28:12-16, that Tyre had as one of her symbols or cognizances some cherubic device. The King of Tyre, in apparently a taunting message, is called *"the anointed cherub,"* and *"the covering cherub,"* and we find a winged lion the cognizance of Venice. Again, Tyre, the capital of *Phoenicia*, was the proud merchant city of ancient times, and Venice, the capital of *Venetia*, held the same grand position in the middle ages. Is there not in addition some clear connection between Venetia and *Phoenicia*?

From Venetia we will return to the Dan-astris (Dniester), follow it to its source, where we pick up the Vistula, at the mouth of which is *Dan*-zig on the shores of the Co-*dan* Gulf (now the Baltic), across to *Dan*nemora, opposite the Gulf of Finland, down the Baltic to *Dan*nemerk, the country of our beloved Princess; across the North Sea to the Humber, where we find the river *Don*, and go south to Don-caster. Then we find a whole county *Dan*nonia, now Devonshire, and from thence we may cross to that undisputed head-quarters of the *Dannans*, the North of Ireland, anciently called Scotia, where we find an immense percentage not only of the names of places, but of the popular surnames with the prefix Don: *Dun*dalk, *Don*egal and *Don*aghadee. This last place, if not the earliest, is one of the earliest reputed settlements of the Tuath de Dannan: it had a sound remarkably Hebrew, and transliterated becomes הֵעָדִי דָן Danhaghedee, "Dan my witness." From ancient Scotia we pass over to modern Scotia, or Cale-*don*-ia, whose namesake we had in Greece. Here, among a host of others, we have *Dum*fries, *Dum*barton (in these the letter *n* becomes *m* before the labial), *Dun*dee, and Aber*deen* (mouth of the *Don*), and the river *Don*.

CHAPTER II

DANAI OF GREECE ARE DANNITES OF ISRAEL

Reputed Egyptian origin of both – Chronology agrees–Grecian Danai called *Argives* – Latham's opinion – Phoenician connections of both – Argive Danai also called *Heraclidae* – Lacedaemonians are Argives and Heraclidae – Serpent and Eagle symbols common to both – Egyptian monuments in serpent worship refer to both, by Dr. Brugsch – The Macedonians or their ruling families were Argive Danai – Serpent and Eagle symbols of Alexander the Great and his Generals – Lacedaemonians (*i.e.*, Danai Heraclidae) – Their eagle serpent seal – Acknowledged by Jewish High Priest to be their *"brethren of the stock of Abraham."*

Having now given a general view of our field of operations, as marked by the names attaching to rivers and countries, let us see how history and various marks favour the identification of these footprints as belonging to Dannites of *Israel* as identical with the Danai of Greece.

In history the renowned Danai of Greece are foremost. Danaus, it tells us, came from Egypt; so did Israel. And Jethro's daughters, speaking of Moses, told their father *"an Egyptian delivered us."* (Exod. 2:19) Strabo, who lived between 40 B.C. and 20 A.D., says (xvi. ii. 34, 35), *"the Egyptians were the ancestors of the present Jews."* Apion, an Egyptian priest in the first century B.C., calls the Israelites renegade Egyptians. And thus it serves the purpose of identification well that Danaus of Grecian history should be represented as coming from Egypt. The Danai are mentioned by Homer Pindar, Euripides, Strabo, and others. When we talk of

Homer, and the still earlier times of which he sang, we are apt to think that these are so early that we could have no earlier records; but it will be well to refresh our memories with dates. – The siege of Troy, then, whose heroes on both sides Homer has immortalised, is believed to have taken place about 1193 B.C.; but Deborah and Barak taunted Dan with getting his ships nearly 100 years before that, or 1285 B.C.; and the conquest of the Holy Land by Joshua was a century and a half before that again, or about 1443 B.C.! The various dates assigned to the arrival of Danaus in Argos would place that event at from fourteen years to two hundred *later* than the conquest of the Holy Land.

According to Euripides and Strabo: *"Danaus having arrived in Argos made a law that those who had borne the name of Pelasgiotoe throughout Greece should be called Danai."* (Strabo v.ii. 4) Compare this with the act of the people of Dan (Judges 18:29). We learn from Strabo and others that this Argos soon spread its name to the Pelonnesus, and afterwards to all Greece, for he says (viii. 6, 5), *"Homer calls the whole of Greece Argos, for he calls all Argives, as he calls them Danai and Achoei."*

"I think," says Latham (*Ethnology of Europe*, p. 157), "that the eponymus of the Argive Danai was no other than that of the Israelite Tribe of Dan, only we are so used to confining ourselves to the soil of Palestine in our consideration of the Israelites, that we treat them as if they were *adscripti gleboe*, and ignore the share they may have taken in the ordinary history of the world. The sea ports between Tyre and Ascalon, of Dan, Ephraim, and Ashur, must have followed the history of sea ports in general, and not have stood on the coast for nothing. What a light would be thrown on the origin of the name Peloponnesus and the history of the *Pelop-id* family if a *bona fid* nation of *Pelopes*, with unequivocal affinities and contemporary annals, had existed on the coast of Asia! Who would have hesitated to connect the two? Yet with the Danai and the Tribe of Dan this *is* the case, and no one connects them!"

To revert to Argos, this head of all Greece, the first city of the Danai, it stood with two others, Mycene and *Tiryns*, the latter of which, standing as it does close to the city of the Danai, *might* derive its name from *Tyre*. There is another instance of the kind, the Danaster (Dniester) is sometimes called the *Tyras* (Herod. iv. 51; Strabo vii, i. 1), and the people living there are called *Tyritae*. It is reasonable to infer that, from the intimate home relations of the people of Tyre with the Dannites of Israel, the names of Tyre and Dan were used indiscriminately.

Argos is said by the Greeks to have been the birthplace of Hercules, but Herodotus, who went to some trouble to find out who Hercules really was, made a special voyage to Tyre (ii. 44) and found an older Temple to Hercules.

The origin of the Grecian Hercules, or rather *Heracles* as it is in Greek, seems to me to have been in the daring adventures and exploits of the semi-traders and buccaneers of Tyre and Dan, out of which they formed an ideal man suitable to that heroic age, and in apparent conformity with the earliest Divine command (Gen. 1:26, 28) to *"subdue"* and *"have dominion."* In Hebrew *rakal* means to trade and *Heracleem* means traders.* Those who went forth from Argos and subdued other parts of Greece are spoken of as *Heraclidae*, or *descendants of Heracles*. For a while, apparently in the confusion caused by the Trojan War, they were driven northward out of the Peloponnesus, of which some years after they made a re-conquest, which was called "the return of the descendants of Hercules." (see Muller's *History of the Dorians*) From these are the Lacedaemonians, whose capital was Sparta. Thus Agamemnon, who was chosen Commander-in-Chief of all the Greeks proceeding to the siege of Troy, was King of Argos and Mycene, and his brother, Menelaus, was King of Sparta, capital of Lacedaemon.

---

* אַרְגָּז Argoz also, from רָגַז ragoz, *to move*, is Hebrew for *"a portable chest,"* a name which might well symbolize *trade* or *commerce* (so *Argosy, a merchant ship*). And the reputed mother of Heracles, *Alcmene* (whose name is sometimes applied to Minerva

goddess of *Science*), seems likely to be the Hebrew כימה chymeh, *heat* or *warmth*, as a producing or loosening power, with the particle אל al, as in Arabic, *Alchymy*. This seems the more probable as this Alcmene was said to be the daughter of *Electryon*, derived from the Greek word for *amber*, by rubbing which *electric* sparks are produced; known certainly to Thales, a so-called Phoenician, circ. 600 B.C. But the Greek word *elektron* seems derived from the Hebrew קטר keter, *to fume, to make to smoke*; as a noun, *vapour, incense* (for which amber, which gives a pungent aromatic smoke, was largely used), also with the particle אל al. The foundation of the whole may be, that at Thebes, in Boeotia, the adopted country of Cadmus the Phoenician, was a college in *science*, Alcmene, which the aspiring young Dannites, sons of the enterprising traders or Herakleem of Argos, called their *mother*.

Herodotus (iv. 147) calls Theras regent of Lacedaemon, a *Cadmoean* and *Phoenician*. But, with this confused assignment of Egyptian and Phoenician origin, which admirably suits the Israelites, we have this fact prominent, that a people *called Danai arrived in Argos and extended their rule to all Greece, and that the Lacedaemonians, whether as Argives or Heraclidae, were the most notable branch from this place.* To this point I shall have to refer again.

THE TRIBE OF DAN

But again: We will try to identify these Grecian Danai by their symbols. The serpent is held by various Hebrew and Chaldee writers to have been the cognizance of Dan: *"Dan shall be a serpent in the way, an adder in the path,"* said Jacob (Gen. 49:17). The serpent was an emblem of sin as well as of wisdom and subtility (*Be ye wise as serpents*), and the patriarch may have foreseen that this Tribe would be the first to lapse into idolatry. At any rate, this fact has not escaped Jewish or Gentile writers. As head of three Tribes – *i.e.*, one of the four camps – Dan had also the eagle, one of the four cherubic symbols, and hence the two signs are often combined. *"Ancient learned Jewish authorities unanimously assert that Dan bore scorpio under an eagle."* (Mazzaroth 39) *"Ancient Hebrew and Chaldee authorities say that Dan bore on his standard a crowned serpent or basilisk held in the claws of an eagle."* (Mazzaroth 41)

Of the four evangelists, St. John's emblem is the eagle, and in many of the representations of him the serpent also is introduced. His mission was chiefly, if not entirely, among the Greeks. St. John's symbol also sometimes takes the form of a dragon, a compound of the serpent with the eagle and lion; for Dan was also called by his father *"a lion's whelp."*

As regards the employment of these symbols among the Greeks, I find in *Wedgewood's Book of Remembrance*, i, 175: "Cecrops, the founder and first king of Athens (also said to have come from Egypt, and who founded twelve cities), was said to have been half a man and half a *serpent*. It is said in another account that the first king of Athens was a dragon, which symbol was borrowed by the Romans from Greece."

In a coin of Athens, a female figure in a chariot is drawn by two *serpents*. (*Calmet's Dict.* V. Athens, 19)

The oracle at Delphi, being consulted by the people of Argos (*Herod.* vi. 77), speaks of the Argives as "the triple-coiled *serpent*," referring probably to the three cities of Argos, Mycene, and Tiryns.

We also find the eagle prominent in Greece:

Woolridge, Drawings from Gems, London, 1868. No. 161 is Jupiter Tonans enthroned with sceptre, the eagle at his side on the ground, from an engraved crystal gem.

Calmet's Dict. V. Ashtaroth 3, Greek coin with an eagle. The celebrated statue of Zeus, sitting enthroned in the Temple at Olympia, held a sceptre tipped with an *eagle*. ("Saturday Magazine," 1840, xvi., 51. Lempriere Jupiter, 382)

The eagle was regarded by the Greeks as the minister or attendant of Jupiter, as if the Dannites, who probably introduced the symbol, might have regarded themselves as God's executive. Jove's sceptre, the emblem of authority and rule, was, as Dan might have thought befitted himself, tipped with the *eagle*.

The eagle is sometimes represented as holding the fulmen or thunderbolt in its claws. This might have been corrupted by the Greeks from Dan's *eagle* holding the *serpent*.

At Baalbec, which was the limit of Joshua's conquests (Josh. 11:17), and which, if not occupied by Dan, was not far from his northern portion, is the so-called Phoenician Temple. It is described in *University History*, vol. ii, 266, and in "Notes of a Clerical Furlough," Dr. Buchanan, *Sunday at Home*, 1862, p. 743: "The Temple appears to have been covered and embellished with eagles. On looking up when under the portal, you see the bottom of the lintel enriched with a piece of sculpture hardly to be equalled. It is a vast eagle carrying in its claws two serpents entwined about a rod."*

---

*The symbol of Marseilles, the ancient so-called Phoenician Massilia, is a figure resembling Britannia. She holds a trident, and wears a breastplate on which is an eagle surrounded by serpents.

Alexander the Great, of Macedon, represented himself to be the son of Jupiter in the form of a *serpent*. Ptolemy (a Hebrew name, better recognized when *Bar* is prefixed) and Seleucus, Alexander's generals, were also Make-don-ians, and their medals all bear the eagle.

But we find that the Make-don-ians were Argives. One of their princes (*Herod.* v. 22) wished to take part in the Olympian games, in which only Greeks could compete. His right was at first disputed, but he successfully proved before the judges that the Make-don-ians were Argives.

It is here worthy of notice that Alexander the Great showed great respect for the Jews; and, on being met before Jerusalem by the Jewish high priest in his robes, declared that he had seen in a dream his counterpart, by whom he was directed to undertake the expedition. (Josephus' *Antiq.* xi. viii. 5)

Tracing still further the serpent symbol, we find the antiquities of Egypt yielding their testimony to the identity of the Grecian Danai with Israelitish Dan. It is worthy of note that Danaus, who is recorded as landing in Greece from Egypt, was said to be the son of Belus, sometimes spelt *Bela*, which strongly resembles *Bilhah*, the name of Jacob's concubine and mother of Dan. (Gen. 30:4-6)

Now Dr. Brugsch, writing on the Exodus of the Israelites, gives us this information, which I extracted from the *Jewish Chronicle* of Jan. 21st, 1876. He discovers –

> "a city name Pi-tom, with the addition of the Egyptian monuments *"in the district of Succoth,"* and that the city is *Tanis*, or *Zoan*. The same place is also called Pi-Rameses. Pitom and Rameses, however, are the places where the Israelites were forced to build the treasuries or storehouses for their oppressors."

Before proceeding, I would remark upon this city, *Tanis* or *Zoan*. The Hebrew **צ**, used in the *Zoan* of the Bible (Psa. 78:12), is convertible into Z, S, D, or T. In the Greek and Latin, for instance, we have Zeus, Deus, and Theos.* So that the city may be called *Tanis* or *Doan*; and in the Black Sea we have the river *Tanais* or *Don*‡

---

*So also: Heb., Tzor; Eng., Tyre; Greek, indifferently, Sor and Turos (see Septuagint Ezek. 27:2, and 28:2); and modern Arabic, Sur.

‡The *oa* in *Tzoan,* and the suggested *Doan,* may have been pronounced as in *loan, moan, roan,* or perhaps a little bro*dd*er.

But to continue the quotation:

"As most of the places of this region can *only* be *derived from the Hebrew*, just like Succoth, it is clear that in these very regions the land of Gosen must be sought. The name Pi-tom denotes city of (the god) *Tom. Tom,* however, add the inscriptions, is also called Ankh, with the surname *the Great God.* Investigation shows that *Ankh* denotes *'the Living One,'* and is nothing else than the Egyptian translation of the Hebrew *Jehovah* or *Jahve. As a symbol of this God a serpent was worshiped in Pitom.* This reminds us of the brass serpent of Moses, and of its worship, which only Hezekiah abolished."

I would rather suggest that *the serpent, as the cognizance of Dan, was the symbol of that city, one of whose names was Tanis,* and eventually became corrupted as the emblem, or similitude, of the God of Dan. But, be this as it may, the locality ascribed to this Israelitish serpent worship in Egypt is the locality from which the Grecian Danai are said to have come.‡

---

‡Dr. Schliemann's collection in the South Kensington Museum of Antiquities, unearthed at Mycene and Argos, is worthy of notice. Models in pottery of some of his metal vases are sold about London. One of these, said to be a flower vase, is of most elegant shape. The handles are the neck, head, and wings of a winged horse, which, it has been conjectured, signifies *migration*. There are two or three small well-known Egyptian symbols – the

owl and scarabaeus – but the principal figures are cherubic; on one side two human-headed lions and an eagle-headed man; and on the other side two human-headed lions and an ox-headed man. Could these be relics of the Danai? Egyptologists would probably say that these were a portion of the Egyptian mythology. It might be so, but they might also as readily have been borrowed from the Israelites as the worship of Jehovah under the form of a serpent, suggested by Dr. Brugsch.

Taken in connection with the many common affinities and symbols already described, the crowning proof of the Identity of the Dannites of Israel with the Danai of Greece lies in the claim of relationship with the Jews preferred by the Lacedaemonians, the most important branch of the Argive Danai, which claim was duly admitted by the high priest at Jerusalem.

It is recorded in I Maccabees xii., and Josephus' *Antiq*. xii. iv. 10, that, about 180 years B.C., the King of the Lacedaemonians sent the following letter to the Jews in Jerusalem:

"Areus, King of the Lacedaemonians, to Onias, the High Priest, sendeth greeting. It is found in writing that the Lacedaemonians and Jews are brethren, and that they are of the stock of Abraham. Now, therefore, since this has come to our knowledge, ye shall do well to write unto us of your prosperity."

They give no clue or hint as to what the relationship might be, except (recorded by Josephus only) calling attention to the seal: "The letter is four-square, and the seal is an eagle with a dragon in its claws" – the cognizant, in fact, of Dan. Now the Jews are stated by Josephus to have replied thus:

"We joyfully received the epistle, and were well pleased with Demoteles and Araeus, although we did not need such a demonstration, because we were well satisfied about it from the *sacred writings*." (Josephus xiii. v. 8)

Did the Jews allude to Ezek. 17:19, where Dan is represented in company with Greece trading to Tyre?

CHAPTER III

DAN IN THE BLACK SEA

Jason's expedition – Thessalians, so-called Phoenicians, who composed it, were also Heraclidae and Argives – *i.e.*, Danai – The Colchians, descendants of the Argonauts, acknowledged as relatives by the Lacedaemonians – Colchians, in Herodotus' time, observed circumcision – Towns of Jason, Median helmet – Divine forethought – "My sanctified ones" – Halor and Habor, Colchians and Iberians – "Elect of the dispersion" – Tumuli and serpent worship – Indian rock records of Dan and other Tribes of Israel, probably in Media, attacked by Cyrus.

It was, as nearly as chronologists can determine, about B.C. 1280 when Jason's expedition, composed of the flower of Thessaly, sailed in the *Argo* from the port of Iolchos. To compare dates: this expedition took place about 160 years *later* than Joshua's conquest of Canaan, about 150 years later than Danaus' first colony in Argos, and about five years later than when Deborah and Barak taunted Dan with keeping on board ship.

The Thessalians are Heraclidae, for Thessalus was a mythical son of Heracles. Now Thessaly, Strabo tells us (ix. ii. 3), was colonized by Phoenicians (so called). He also tells us (v. ii. 4) that it was Argive; hence we come round again to the Danai. There is an additional tallying proof also of their being genuine Danai, for, many years afterwards, a shipload of the descendants of the Argonauts found their way back to Greece (Strabo viii, iii. 19; Herod. iv. 145), and claimed relationship with the Lacedaemonians, whom they called "their fathers"; and the claim was admitted.

– To return to the Argonauts. Their object is shrouded in mythic legend, but it was probably some buccaneering enterprise. Heracles is said to have been on board; and they sailed to the eastern extremity of the Black Sea, and founded Colchis, the modern Poti.

Herodotus (ii. 104) mentions the important fact that in his time, B.C. 420, the Colchians observed circumcision.* He adds: "I found that the Colchians had more recollection of the Egyptians than the Egyptians had of the Colchians." Israel, indeed, would long retain a very lively recollection of the Egyptians! He also says (ii. 105): "The Colchians alone, and the Egyptians, manufacture linen in the same manner, and the whole way of living and the language is similar in both nations; but the Colchian linen is called by the Greeks sar*don-ic*,‡ though that which comes from Egypt is called Egyptian."

---

*Herodotus adds: "The *Syrians* about Thermodon (a river running into the Black Sea), and the river Parthenius, with their neighbours the Macrones, confess that they very lately learnt the same custom from the Colchians." Thus there was a genuine colony direct from Syria in these parts. Now Josephus, on this very passage in Herodotus, denies that any inhabitants of Palestine, except Jews, practice circumcision (Joseph. agst. Apion i. 22). Instead of *learning* it from the Colchians, these emigrants from Syria possibly *returned to the covenant* at the *instigation*, or through the *example*, of the Colchians.

‡ זָר *zar* (from זרה *to scatter, disperse*), one *alienated*, a *stranger* "who had been as it were *scattered* at a distance, or *cast away* from others" (Parkhurst Lex.); in fact, *detached* or *emigrant*. Thus Sar-don-i and Sar-din-i would mean *emigrant, dispersed*, or *detached* Dannites; and Sar-don-ik, anything made by, or pertaining to, them.

These Argonauts – reinforced, perhaps, by fresh batches of their countrymen – pioneered their way inland, for Strabo (xi. xiiv. 12-14, and i. ii. 39) says: "Traces of Jason's expedition still remain, and the Jasonica, or towns of Jason, are every where met with in Armenia,

Media, and the surrounding countries." The Median helmet, we are told by several writers, was *serpent-crested*. Might this not have been introduced among the race by these Dannite colonists? At any rate, even here the Bible does not leave us without a witness to God's providence. In Isa. 12, which calls the hosts together for the punishment of Babylon, the banner for their assembly is to be lifted *"upon the high mountain" – i.e.*, the mountains of Armenia – whence the scourge came: the first called are *"My sanctified ones"* (ver. 2, 3). In the 17th verse, the Medes are mentioned; but who but Israel could be called God's *"sanctified ones"?* What then? Why, it shows that, 500 years before Israel's captivity, God, who foresaw Israel's sin and necessary punishment, was still providing for Israel's safety and comfort by having the country – to which as wretched, degraded captives they would eventually be brought – pioneered, opened up for them, and settled by batches of their more adventurous brethren the Dannites; and secondly, that, while using Babylon as a scourge against Judah, who had gone after Babylonish gods, God was secretly fostering in the mountains of Media, north of Babylon, a rod of His own *"sanctified ones":* an offshoot of Israel, wherewith to destroy Babylon for her cruelty towards His people. These "sanctified ones" in Media may give us a clue to the ancestry of that remarkable man, Cyrus, whom God calls *"Mine anointed."* (Isa. 45:1) (See note p. 33).

Sir Isaac Newton (*Chron. Anct. Hist.*, p. 283), and most other writers on the subject, take Halah and Habor (II Kings 18:11) to be Colchis and Iberia. Allatius supposes that the Israelites who were placed on the Chaborras also peopled the countries of Iberia and Colchis; and he adduces the authority of Constantine Porphyrogenetes in support of the Israelitish origin of the inhabitants of Iberia. The name Iberia, as well as Bithynia – also on the south coast of the Black Sea – certainly strike one as of Hebrew origin.

Again, I find in Ezra 8:17 that, on the return from the seventy years', or Babylonish, captivity, having no Levites, Ezra had to send to *"Iddo, the chief of the place Casiphia, that they should bring unto us ministers for the house of God."* And in Dr. Henderson's Russian researches, Casiphia is identified as a district bordering on the Caspian.

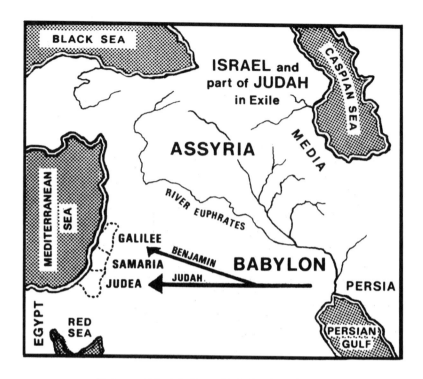

Return of Judah from Babylonian Captivity

In the times of the apostles it was recognized that members of the Ten Tribes were in Asia Minor, for St. Peter's first epistle is addressed, *not* to the *"strangers scattered,"* &c., as in our translation, but "to the elect strangers" (in the sense of *strangers and pilgrims*) OF THE DISPERSION (see the Greek and Alford's notes on this passage); *"the dispersion"* being the word used by the Jews denoting the Ten tribes.

Josephus states (*Antiq.* xi. v. 2) that when Ezra received permission to return to Jerusalem and rebuild the temple, "he sent a copy of the epistle to all of his own nation that were in *Media.*" He adds, "But then *the entire body of the people of Israel* remained in that country, wherefore there are but Two Tribes in Asia and Europe subject to the Romans, while the Ten Tribes are beyond Euphrates till now, and are an *immense multitude and not to be estimated by numbers.*"

Of the region of Colchis, Dr. Clarke mentions the vast number of *tumuli* which he thinks must be placed as marks for guidance across the immense plains, and they continue on to the sea of Azov; "reminding us of the prophet's warning to exiled Israel, *'Set thee up waymarks.'*" I have observed the same on the Danube, where tumuli stretch from Widdin in a southeast direction, apparently towards the Gulf of Burgas: a few are visible on the north bank stretching towards the northwest.

The Russian Archaeological Society opened one of these tumuli near Poti. Within was a large arched vault beautifully constructed of white limestone, in which was found a gold serpent with ruby eyes. Now the Beni-Israel of India secretly worship a serpent of this sort, generally of silver. (Carpenter, 42)

The rock temples of India give us some additional testimony regarding the existence, in the regions about the Black Sea, of the Dannites and other Tribes of Israel. (The Cyrus mentioned is probably the one who was killed in an expedition against the Massagetae.) From the preface of Moore's *Saxons of the East and West,* I extract the following translation of a Hebraic inscription upon the walls of a rock temple in Kanari, twenty miles north of Bombay:

> "Lo the worship of Saka is the fruit of my lip. His garden, which Cyrus laid low, was glowing red, behold it is blackened. His people being aroused would have their rights; for they were cast down at the cry of the parting of Dan, who being delivered was perfectly free . . . . Everyone grew mighty, and Saka's mouth enkindling them brought the princes together of the race of Harari (people of the hill country of Ephraim, so-called – II Sam. 23:9-11). As to Dan, his unloosing was destruction, oppression, and strife. He stoutly turned away; he departed twice. The pre-determined thought is a hand prepared: yea, Gotha (*i.e.,* the opposite or north coast of the Black Sea called Gothland), that watched for the presence of Dan afforded concealment to the exile . . . . The redeemed of Kasha wandered about like a flock over-driven." (See note pp. 32-33)

This name *Saka*, used in the inscriptions apparently as a title of their God, is one of the titles signifying *"the most pure,"* given to God in the Jewish Passover hymn at the present day. The people who used it were in company with Dan, and, as it is Hebraic, and an allusion seems to be made to the princes of Ephraim, they were probably the descendants of the captivity of Samaria (II Kings 17:6), and of Reuben, Gad, and the half Tribe off Manasseh (II Kings 15:29), who had had some two centuries to increase and expand. Might they not also be identical with the Sakai or Scythians, who about this time possessed those regions? The Persians called all the Scythians, Sakai. The *Jewish Chronicle*, 24th March, 1876, mentions the *Zaccai* as one of the oldest family names among the Jews of Cochin remaining to this day.

I shall in the next chapter endeavour to show the Israelitish affinities of these Sakai or Scythians, and their connection with the Danai.

In the historical facts which I have brought forward and endeavoured to connect, there is one point which needs explanation before the subject of this chapter is dismissed. It will occur to many to ask, why, assuming the Lacedaemonians, Thessalians, and Colchins to be Danites of Israel, should there be traces of circumcision among the Colchains only? The answer is, that the Dannite element was probably in many places a comparative handful, more or less, of the clever, enterprising, determined set of spirits, bred in the wilderness under Moses, and inured to war, which imposed its rule* and name on inferior and more primitive races. This would seem to account for the "descendants of Heracles" being sometimes compelled to fly their countries, and make a fresh muster ere they could get back again. The colony of Danaus in Argos was avowedly such a handful, reinforced it may be afterwards. The other colonies were probably the same; and, had the Macedonian people *generally* been Argives,‡ it would have been too well known and admitted for any doubt to have been raised at the Olympian games when one of their princes (Herod. v. 22) was compelled to prove his Argive descent ere he was permitted to enter the lists.

I assume that the Colchians, as descended from the Argonauts, the best blood of Thessaly, were composed chiefly, if not altogether, of this Hebrew stock, and that, while this strengthened their position in Colchis, and favoured the retention of their racial customs in that remote corner, it impoverished the Hebrew blood left in Greece, where those customs which were peculiar to Israelites, and of no apparent general utility or interest, disappeared, as Greece became a centre of attraction for various races in an age of progress.‡ And thus I think it was that the Colchians retained circumcision until the time of Herodotus, while the Lacedaemonians, when claiming relationship with the Jews, could only refer to their ancient writings and their zeal.

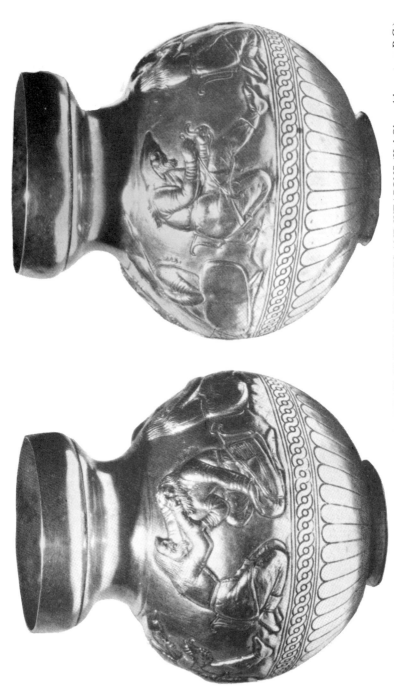

GREEK-MADE ELECTRUM VASE SHOWING SCYTHIAN COSTUME, FEATURES AND WEAPONS (Kul Oba - 4th century B.C.)

CHAPTER IV

DAN AMONG THE SCYTHIANS

Question of circumcision – Scuthi, or Seythian, is Hebrew for wanderers, or those living in temporary dwellings – Were considered Heraclidae by the Greeks – Scythian account, and date of their first appearance as a nation – Place and date of their appearance, according to historians – Their character – The Saka, or Sakai, and Gimiri, or Beth-Kumri of Media – Scythian nation on the north of the Black Sea – King Saulios – *Gruph* and Ch'ruv – Language – Scythian gods are Syro-Phoenician – Goths, Roman name for Scythians – Arsareth – Sacasuni and Saxons.

Although the subject is still, like the previous chapter, "The Danai, or Dan in the Black Sea," let us now more especially examine their connection with the Scythians, or Sakai, for at the close of the previous chapter, we had heard, through the Bombay inscriptions, of Dan, who had been living among the *"people of Saka"* (evidently in Media and Armenia), "unloosing" to cross over to Gothland (the north coast of the Black Sea), when Cyrus came against them. And to the "towns of Jason," in Media and Armenia, we had traced step by step as the Danai of Greece, and Heraclidae or traders, the Colchians, who observed circumcision, the relatives of the Lacedaemonians, who showed the cognizance of Dan, the acknowledged literal *"brethren"* of the Jews. We have also seen that Armenia and Media were the countries to which the Tribes of Israel were deported by the kings of Assyria, and it is north of the Black Sea that in Herodotus' time we find the greater part of the Scythian nation located. It is there also that we find many of the rivers impressed with the name of Dan, the Don or Tanais, the Dan-apris, Dan-astris, and Dan-ube.

Who, then, were the Scythians, these new friends and companions, whom the enterprising Danai have met with in Asia? It would occupy a separate pamphlet of considerable dimensions to adduce all that might be said of the Scythians, as including, if not mainly composed of, the exiled and *"escaped"* of Israel. Some years ago I printed a small paper, *"Our Scythian Ancestors Identified with Israel,"* but the sixteen pages which composed it might be expanded to sixty with evidence of the first importance which has subsequently cropped up. I will therefore only touch upon a few of the leading points.

First, I think the question may be repeated by some readers, "If the Scythians were Israel, *why is there no record of circumcision being observed among them, as stated of the Colchians"*? To this I reply, the Colchians were free emigrants at a comparatively early date, when everything was fresh among the Israelites; whereas Israel's deportation took place between five and six centuries later as a punishment, *not for keeping the law and the covenant, but for breaking them, and for going after other gods and copying the rites of other nations.*

The wonder is not that the Israelites should have relinquished circumcision, but that any portion of them, as the Colchians, should have retained it. For St. Peter speaks of it as *"a yoke which neither we nor our fathers were able to bear"* (Acts 15:10), and during the forty years in the wilderness, under Moses, it was wholly neglected. (Josh. 5:2-9)

Mr. H. P. Smith (*Ancient History of the East,* p. 472) and Professor Rawlinson (*Herodotus,* note on the Scythians) concur in stating that *Scyth* is not a real ethnic name, but a title given to all *nomads,* or *wandering* pastoral tribes.

Now in Hebrew alone does this word mean *wanderers,* and it is connected with one of their most important feasts, the only one apparently which is to be retained after the restoration of all things – viz., the Feast of Tabernacles, or סֻכּוֹת, *Scotch* or *Scot* (booths), which was instituted to commemorate Israel's *wanderings* in the wilderness. (see Lev. 23:40-43; Zech. 14:16; Gen. 33:17) In Hebrew, the dwellers in booths are סֻכּוֹתִי, *Scuthi*, or Scoti, or as we should say, *Succothites*.

Now the Greeks adopted the word, possibly imported by the Danites, and spoke of the Σκυθαι, *Skuthai*, which, through the Latin, we call *"Scythian."* But the Greeks can assign no meaning to the word, but say that these Skuthai were descended from a certain *Skuthees*, who was a mythical son of Heracles and a half *serpent* mother. (*Herod.* iv. 8) Here, then, Greek legend assigns a connection between the Scythians and the Heraclidae, or Danai, and traces of the *serpent are again apparent.* There seems somewhat also of a correspondence in the legends of the Scythians and the Lacedaemonians. The Scythians say that their ancestor was Targetaus, a son of Jupiter by the daughter of a river, (*Herod.* iv. 5) while the Lacedaemonians say that Lacedaemo was the son of Jupiter and Mount *Taygetus*, or *Taygeta.** (See appendix, "What the Scythians said to Herodotus.")

---

*As *"Scythian," "Scuthi,"* or *"Skuthai,"* merely means *"dwellers in booths"* – i.e., nomads – the name, though Hebrew, does not necessarily determine the ethnic affinities of those to whom it was applied, except when accompanied by other evidence. Herodotus often distinguishes between the Scythians *proper*, and Tribes living among them having Scythian *habits*, but who were not Scythian by tradition or language. He speaks of the Scythian *nation* as "very learned" but of certain tribes as dreadful barbarians. Strabo likewise quotes several authors who speak of the excellent laws and habits of the Sakai, a tribe of Scythians who are called *"a righteous race."* The name Saka is a better guide, even though the Persians applied Sakai to all *Scythians*, and Gumri or Gimiri (p. 33), is still more remarkable. But however great the medley, the blood of Abraham, and the effect of the discipline in the wilderness and general training of Israel would soon show up when in contact with mere vagrant vagabond tribes. *"The laws, customs, and* *manners of the Scythians,"* says Epiphanius, *"were received by the other nations as the standards of policy, civility, and polite learning."*

The legendary date of their first appearance under a king in the wilderness (*Herod.* iv. 5-7), 1,000 years before Darius' expedition (500 B.C.), corresponds with the date of Israel under Moses *in the wilderness.*

The date assigned by historians to their first appearance on the Araxes in Media as a *despicable* people (*Diod.* ii. 3) accords with the date of Israel's deportation to those regions by the kings of Assyria.

For their rapid growth and expansion, their excellent laws, their learning, and abhorrence of swine, see Dodorus, Herodotus, Strabo, AEschylus, Epiphanius, &c.

"The Persians," says Herodotus, (vii, 64), "call all the Scythians Sakai." Strabo, (xi., vii. 4), mentions "the Sakai got possession of the most fertile tract of Armenia, which was called after their own name Saccassena." Pliny, (vi. 16), mentions that the Sakai were the most distinguished Scythians, and that those who settled in Armenia were called Saccassani. Ephorus quotes Choerilus, who calls the Sakai of Asia "a colony of nomads, a righteous race."

In a short chapter, iv., of a small pamphlet, "Are We Israelites?" by the Rev Bourchier Wrey Savile, M.A., these Sakai are traced by the aid of Sir H. Rawlinson's own interpretations of the Assyrian inscriptions, to the Ten Tribes of Israel, including the people of Samaria, Beth Kumri, who were carried away by Tiglath-Pileser and Sargon, circ. 721 B.C.

Sir H. Rawlinson, in his brother's edition of *Herodotus*, seems to consider Scyth and Sacan identical in meaning as *Nomads. Scyth*, we have seen, does in the Hebrew mean *"wanderers;"* but in the *Achoemenian inscriptions, Saka,* which Sir Henry calls Aryan, and which he says is replaced by "Gimiri in the Babylonian transcripts of the Persian and Scythic columns,"* refers, I would suggest, either to the worship of God under the title, still extant among the Jews, of Saka, the most pure, or else it is one of their own names, Tsaki, Isaacites or Beth-Isaac, House of Isaac. (See Amos 7:9, 16)

---

*This Gimiri, of the Babylonian transcripts, says Sir H. Rawlinson, *"elsewhere always means the Tribes,"* and is "the Semitic equivalent of the Aryan name of Saka." . . . "The Sacae (Sakai) or Scythians, first appears in the Cuneiform inscriptions about 648 B.C." Now Cyrus's father was *"of the Royal Tribe of Pasar-gadoe,"* of the family of Achoemenes, and his mother was daughter of the Median King Astyages (said to have been the Ahasuerus of Scripture). Cyrus, collecting some of the Tribes called *Persian*, including his own, and aided by a portion of the Medes, overthrew Astyages, and subsequently, with Medes and Persians, advanced against Babylon, circ. 560 B.C. Now in Isaiah 12:3,17, it is the Lord's *"sanctified ones"* who, *together with the Medes*, advance against Babylon under Cyrus, *the Lord's "Shepherd,"* (Isaiah 44:28) and *"Anointed."* (Isaiah 45:1) (See inscriptions regarding the Beth Khumri captives from Samaria, *Records of the Past*, v, pp. 28,41.) If this Cyrus (for Xenophon gives a different account) was afterwards killed in an expedition against the Scythians, he was probably endeavouring to coerce *all the Tribes* into obedience, and to consolidate a new Israelitish empire under a despotism, which would have checked their development. (See pp. 22-25)

Further, as regards the history of the Scythians on the Black Sea, Herodotus, (iv. 76), mentions a king *Saulios*, living on the Danapris (Dnieper). He was father to Idan-Thyrsus, the king who made the irruption against the Medes, and held Asis and the Holy Land for twenty-nine years, penetrating to Egypt. This took place about 630 B.C. – *i.e.*, some eighty or ninety years after the captivity, but nearly 600 years later than Dan's first settlement in the Black Sea: and it reads uncommonly like a wild dash of some of the Tribes – an Israelitish crusade to recover their inheritance.

Herodotus also records (iv. 76) that the Scythians "studiously avoid the use of foreign customs." Now Israel's sin in the Holy Land was too great a fondness for foreign customs, but we may reasonably suppose that the sufferings they had endured and their banishment had brought them somewhat to a sense of their sin, even though they might have been unable to recover the truth. Ezekiel's vision was by the river of Chebar, about 590 B.C., and II Esdras 13:40-42, ascribes as a reason for the Ten Tribes moving away from Media,* that they desired to serve God in their own way.

---

*(See p. 36.) These were probably the *more zealously religious portion* of them, and if, as conjectured, *Arsareth*, where they moved to, be the city or country of the river *Sereth* which flows into the Danube, this would account for the character of the people, the "Dacae called *Polistoe*" who were there in Josephus' time, and whose *strict manner of life* he compares to that of the sect of Essenes among the Jews (*Antiq.* xviii. i. 5): "And I do verily believe are the same with those which Strabo calleth *Plistoe*, and were the stock of the Abii" (a Scythian Tribe whom Arrian calls "the justest people in the world"). – Ortellius Thesaurus, Dacia et Moesia. The Latin *Daci* would be Greek *Dakai*, but (see p. 17) in Hebrew convertible into Z, S, D, or T. The D here used may be the Hebrew tz, and *Dakai* may therefore be corrupted from *Tzaki,* or *Sakai.*

Now it is somewhat remarkable that Herodotus should thus record the jealousy of the Scythians in religious matters (iv. 79, 80). One of their kings named Scylas had in the city of Borysthenes, which was outside his dominions, a large and magnificent mansion; round it were placed sphinxes and *gryphons* of white marble. (Note that the Greek $\gamma\rho\upsilon\psi$, $\gamma\rho\upsilon\phi\varepsilon\varsigma$, *grups, gruphes*, is the Hebrew כרוב, *chr'uv*, or as we say cherub.) Scylas was very desirous of being initiated into the mysteries of Bacchus, but he was afraid of any of his people seeing him. He used, therefore, to go there in private and assume the Greek dress. On the occasion of his initiation, "just as he was about to commence the sacred rites, a very great prodigy occurred. . . . . the god hurled a bolt and his palace was entirely burnt down."‡

---

‡Though the Scythians objected to Bacchanalian orgies in the heathen sense, they appear to have been hard drinkers of "unmixed wine": so that *"pour out like a Scythian"* was a saying among the Spartans when they wanted something stronger. (*Herod.* vi. 84)

Herodotus has also left us two or three specimens of the Scythian language – viz., iv. 27. He says *spou* means *the eye*, which may be from the Hebrew root צָפָה, *tspeh*, to watch, to look around: English *spy*. But the most remarkable one is the following: In iv. 52, he describes "a bitter fountain," which discharges itself into the Hypanis and taints the water. "The name of the fountain is," he says, "in the Scythian language *'Exampoeus,'* but in the language of the Greeks, ἱεροὶ ὁδοὶ *'the sacred ways.'* From this, many writers have inferred that *Exampoeus* is Scythian for *sacred ways*, but Herodotus does not say so. Now I find that in Hebrew פי הסם, *ha-sam-pe*, would mean *the bitter* or *medicinal outlet*: from סם *sam*, meaning as a verb *'to smell,'* and, as a noun, *'drugs,'* *'poison,'* 'bitter,' and פי or פה, *pi* or *per*, *'a well's mouth,'* *'outlet,'* or *'opening.'*"

Again, iv. 59, Herodotus gives a list of the   deities of the Scythians. These have surprised many writers, but the following is the note of the   Rev. J.W. Blakesley, B.D., in the Cambridge Bibliotheca classica edition of *Herodotus*:

Παπαιος –Απια ., These two reputed Scythian words seem to be unquestionably of the *Indio-Germanic* family of languages. Απια is a name by which a portion of the Peloponnesus was anciently called (AEschylus Sup. 260-269), and it is probably identical in etymology with the word ηπια, and originally an epithet of the earth considered as an object of worship ιλεομαι μεν Απιαν ϳουνιν, (Suppl. 117-127). *Artimpasa*, if genuine, seems to be merely another form of *Artemis* with an affix. (Etosyrus is most suspiciously like οιτος Συρος, the *Syrian dirge*, or *chant*, of which the proper name was Linus. Thamimasadas, too, suggests the Tammuz of Ezek. 8:14 in a Hellenic dress. *So that all these names, with the exception of Tabiti – and perhaps that, too, may be the Topheth of II Kings 23:10 – seem to belong to an Achaean or Syro-Phoenician language, and to all appearance are not genuine Scythian.*

If it had occurred to Mr. Blakesley that the Scythians were Israelites who had come via Media, and that, Danites had preceded them many centuries via Greece, he would have understood how these names would naturally bear an Indo-Germanic and Syro-Phoenician stamp, and a Greek dress, and still be Scythian.*

---

*The same might be said of the recent paper by Professor Bugge of Christiana ("the highest living authority") on "The Origin of Norse Mythology." (See *Academy*, Nov. 29, 1879, p. 396) He traces Norse mythology to "tales heard by the Vikings from Englishmen and Irishmen." And these tales are, he says, a mixture of "old Greek-Roman mythology," and "Jewish-Christian Bible legends." Dr. Baug also read a paper on "The Voluspa." If it had occurred to the Professor that the Danite Vikings had met the Irish Danan, Greek Danai, and English Saka in "Gothland on the Euxine," and perhaps before that in Media, he would have seen how they could have become possessed of Jewish-Christian and Greek-Roman tales, *sharing* them *with*, and not *borrowing* them *from*, Englishmen or Irishmen.

The Scythians were later known as Goths, or Gothi, possibly because the Getae, an important branch of the Scythian nation, were

−36−

most in contact with the Romans, with whom, therefore, all Scythians were Gothi. Sailman, a Jewish writer in 1818, in *Researchers in the East* quotes Ortellius, who "notes the kingdom of *Arsareth* (see II Esdras 8:45), where the Ten Tribes, retiring, took the name of *Gauthei*." John Wilson has pointed out that the country of the Getae was on the borders of the Danubian principalities, on the river *Sereth*, where is a town of the same name, which, in the Hebrew tongue, would be *Ar-sereth*. (See note, p. 34.) It is necessary to point out this identity of the Scythians and Goths, and their connection with Danai, for we have Gothland and the Danai in the Black Sea, and again we have Gotha and Gothland in the Baltic, and the Annans, or Danes, again.

As apropos to the general subject, it may be observed in concluding this chapter that Ptolemy mentions a Scythian people sprung from the Sakai, named Saxones. (Sharon Turner, *Anglo-Sax.*, vol. i., p. 100) Also Moore in *Pillar Stones of Scotland* observes:

> "That the Sacasuni of Armenia were of the same stock as the Saxons of England is deemed sufficiently evident by those who have most deeply studied the subject. (See *Origin and Progress of the Scythians or Goths*, by John Pinkerton, 1788; Sharon Turner's *History of the Anglo-Saxons*; and *Les Scythes*, by F. G. Bergmann.)"

SCYTHIAN FIGURE (Gold - 4th century B.C.)

CHAPTER V

DANNANS, OR DANES, OF SCANDINAVIA, IRELAND, AND SCOTLAND

Holsace chronicles – Education – Odin's capital, Asgard – Modern Asgard north of Lake Van – Baal worship and the serpent – IRELAND, Tuatha Danan from Greece and the Euxine – Date of arrival – Poenulus of Plautus – Milesians, Gadelians, or Scoti, from the Euxine – Villaneuva's Phoenician Ireland – Baal worship: serpent and eagle – SCOTLAND, Dannans, Baal worship, coins.

The Danes are always spoken of as the Gothic family (see Otta's *Scandinavia*, and others), though seemingly more specially given to the sea than the other Gothic Tribes. The reputed common ancestor, leader, or deity of Goths, Saxons, and Danes, was one, Odin. The Danes also claim as an ancestor, or leader, a renowned warrior named Dan, and hence their country was called *Danne*-merk, or Dan's-land.

The settlements of the Dannans, or Danes, in Denmark and Norway seem to have been made in very remote times, for the Irish colony of Dannans are said to have visited Denmark first, and to have found their compatriots and namesakes there before them in some strength with considerable towns. It is characteristic of these early Dannans that, wherever we read of them, we hear of their *establishing schools*; and being regarded, of course for their superior knowledge, as magicians by the simpler aborigines of the countries to which they came.

Odin is a historical and mythical personage. It was a name also often assumed by Danish chieftains. In Norse it is *Ottin*, in Gothic

Wuotan, the Lombards wrote *Wodan*, Old Saxons *Wodan*, Westphalian Saxons *Godan*, or *Gudan* (Grimm; Moore's *Pillar Stones of Scotland*, 151, and Sharon Turner, *Anglo-Sax.*, vol. i., p. 100).

> "Odin's capital, Asgard, was supposed to be between the Euxine and Caspian Seas. . . . . The chronicle of the Swedish kings commences with an account of a people on the east of the river Tana-quisl (the Tana-quisl is the Dana-strom, or Danube). The people were governed by a pontiff-king, Odin. These people introduced the worship of Odin into Denmark and Sweden (Moore's *Pillar Stones*, p. 149; see *Traces de Buddhisme en Norvege*, par M. C. A. Holmboe, Professeur de Langues Orientales en Universitie Royale de Norvege)."

From the time of the defection of the Ten Tribes under Jeroboam, the kings of Israel seem to have constituted themselves pontiff-kings. They made the priests, and were priests themselves. (See I Kings 13:1,33) And (whether or not the places be identical) there, in Media, in the exact position assigned to the headquarters of the Ten Tribes (II Esdras 13:43), south of the sources, or *"narrow passages,"* of the Euphrates, may be found, in the best modern maps, the district or province Asgerd, with its capital of the same name, corresponding, as well as can fairly be conceived, with Asgard, the traditional home and palace of Odin, "near the Euxine and Caspian Seas."

The position of Asgerd, in the Prussian map which I possess, is about 30 miles north of Lake Van.

In Norway and Denmark, as in Scotland and Ireland, Baal worship flourished – that old mark of Phoenician company, that pet of Jezebel, wife of King Ahab and daughter of Eth-baal, King of Sidon. (I Kings 16:30,31)

Here also we find almost national the old badge which everywhere we have observed attaching to the Danai, or Danites – the serpent. Numerous Danish families bear it, and it is the most common device in the ancient Danish jewellery.

The old Irish manuscripts, many of which I believe are still untranslated, seem to possess a vast amount of information regarding the Dannans, or Tuath di Dannan, *Tribe of Dannan*. At present Keatinge's, *History of Ireland*, and *Annals of Ireland*, *by the Four Masters*, are I believe the best works. In these histories, compiled from ancient records, the Dannans and Milesians, said to be the same race, are represented as arriving in various batches from Greece, from "Gothland in the Euxine," and from "Scythia near the Euxine and Caspian Seas," and early Phoenician and Egyptian affinities are likewise noticed. Thus they confirm much of the information regarding the various colonies founded by the Danai, which have been traced out through many historians in this paper.

Keatinge's *History of Ireland* states that there were two peoples who arrived in Ireland, the Dannans and Milesians, of whom the Dannans arrived first. At p. 40 he says, "The Dannans were a people of great learning; they had overmuch gold and silver . . . . they left Greece after a battle with the Assyrians, and, for fear of falling into the hands of the Assyrians, came to Norway and Denmark, and thence passed over to Ireland."

From *Annals of Ireland*, *by the Four Masters*, I extract the following note (p. 121):

> "The colony called Tuatha de Dannan conquered the Firbolgs, and became masters of Ireland. It appears that the Dannans were a highly civilized people, far more skilled in arts and sciences than any of the other colonies that settled in Ireland. They ruled in Ireland about two centuries, or 197 years according to the Psalter of Cashel, and were highly skilled in architecture and other arts *from their long residence in Greece and intercourse with the Phoenicians.*"

Again (p. 123), "The Dannans ruled about two centuries, until the arrival of the Milesians, which took place 1,000 years before the Christian era." Thus the date of the arrival of the first colony of the Dannans would be 1200 B.C., or 85 years after Deborah and Barak's victory, when we are told Dan had ships.

Keatinge observes, at p. 30, that the Milesians were the same race as the Dannans, for when the son of Breogan arrived, the people conversed in the same language. What this language was is proved by the words of the Phoenician or Carthagenian slave in the Poenulus of Plautus being nearly pure Irish, as spoken only last century. It is shown in a pamphlet printed in Dublin in 1772, "Essay on the Antiquity of the Irish Language." The Phoenician language was identical with the Hebrew. The same passage in Plautus may be found transliterated into Hebrew in the *Transactions Bib. Arch.*, part ii., 1874.

The Milesians, observes Keatinge, are sometimes called Gadelians, from a leader Gadhol (Hebrew "great"). At p. 72 he states, "The most ancient Irish chronicles assert that the Gadelians in general were called Scots, because they came out of Scythia"; and at p. 76 he says, "Irish records of great antiquity assert that the Gadelians continued in *Gothland in the Euxine* 150 years," after leaving their country, and before going, via Spain, into Ireland.

Annals of Ireland, by the Four Masters, note p. 123: "The Milesians, according to our old annalists, were originally a colony from Scythia, near to the Euxine and Caspian Seas, on the borders of Europe and Asia, and about the country now called the Crimea. From these people, called also Scoti, or Scots, Ireland got the name of Scotia."

Villaneuva's *Phoenician Ireland*, translated by H. O'Brien, p. 184, has the following curious remark accounting for the name Dannan, when endeavouring to prove them Phoenician:

> "I recollect that in the Phoenician language is to be found the word *danihain*, signifying illustrious, generous, noble, or rather Danirfor, Danani, or Danita, *the inhabitants of the city of Dan at the foot of Mount Lebanus, the spot where the Phoenicians (!) worshipped the graven image given them by Micah, and where Jeroboam erected the golden calf!*" (Judges 18:22-31)

It would be endless to attempt to relate all that is said in the Irish records of the Dannans, and that mark of Phoenicia and Israel, Baal worship. The Psalter of Cashel says that the Tower of Tara was built for the preservation of the fire of Baal, and was called Bel Theine. The early connection with Greece, Phoenicia, and Egypt is constantly alluded to throughout the chronicles and records of the Irish Dannans.

I have not observed that the serpent appears among Irish symbols; but Dr. Clarke (*Sunday at Home*, 1862, p. 678) observes that the freedom of Ireland from serpents was attributed to a talisman astrologically formed under the sign Scorpio. Here may be an occult connection between Ireland and Scorpio – Dan's sign.

The eagle, however, does appear. An ancient coin of Ireland was called "an eagle," and the figure of an eagle was impressed upon it. It was current in Edward I's reign, about 1270 A.D.

The mythical bird, the Phoenix, so characteristic of Tyre, is sometimes met with. It is supposed to expire in flames, and rise young again every cycle of 490 years (70 x 7). Its original place is said to have been Heliopolis, or the city of On, in Egypt, one of the most remarkable cities connected with the history of the Israelites.

SCOTLAND

Large bodies of Annans crossed over to Scotland, both from Europe and from Ireland, in very early times. Here also we find numerous traces of Baal worship and Bel Theine, as well as Buddhism. The pillar stones generally bear a serpent.

> "We see the *Phoenician* serpent deity with its head surrounded with a nimbus, or half, as of the sun itself, curiously enough reproduced as one of the supporters to the arms of the Highland clan Donnachie." (Journal Transactions Victoria Institute, 1875; Lecture by J. S. Phene, Esq., LL.D., F.S.A., on "Pre-historic Traditions and Customs in Connection with Sun and Serpent Worship," sec. 18)

Coins of Philip of Macedon, and also of the Brutii in Magna Grecia, were found on the estate of Cairnbulg, in Aberdeenshire, in 1824; a gold coin of Alexander the Great at Ecclefechan,

Dumfrieshire. A large number of Greek coins were found on the farm of Braco, in the parish of Shotto, Lanarkshire: one of Athens, one of Boeotia, and a Parthian coin of Arsaces XI. (*New Statist. Art.*, vol. iv. p. 292, quoted in Wilson's *Pre-historic Annals of Scotland*, vol. ii. p. 313)

The subject of the Dannans in Ireland and Scotland cannot be dismissed without a brief notice of THE CORONATION STONE.

According to the *Annals of Ireland, by the Four Masters*, this stone was brought by the Dannans from the East:

> "Inis Fail, signifying the Island of Destiny, was the name given to Ireland by the Tuatha-di-Dannans, from a remarkable stone they brought with them into Ireland, which was called the Lia-Fail, or Stone of Destiny, sitting on which the ancient kings, both of the Dannan and Milesian race (being the same people), were for many ages crowned at Tara. This stone was sent to Scotland in the sixth century for the coronation of Fergus, King of Scots, who was descended from the Milesian kings of Ireland, and was used for many centuries at the coronation of the Scottish kings, and kept at the Abbey of Scone, from whence it was taken to England by Edward I when he invaded Scotland, and placed under the coronation chair in Westminster Abbey, where it still remains, though it has been erroneously stated in some modern publication that the large pillar stone, which stands on the mound, or rath, at Tara, is the Stone of Destiny, an assertion opposed to the statements of O'Flaherty, the O'Conors, and all other learned antiquarians." . . . "From the ancient Scottish kings of Irish Milesian race were descended the kings of Scotland and royal house of Stewart." – *Note p. 112, by Owen Counellan.*

> "When our king [Edward I] went forth to see the mountains, and, understanding that all was in peace and quiet, he turned to the abbeie of Scone, which was of chanons regular, where he took the stone, called the

Regall of Scotland, upon which the kynges of that nation were wont to sit at the time of their coronations for a throne, and sent it to the Abbeie of Westminster. The Scots dreame that this was the stone whereon Jacob slept when he fled into Mesopotamia." (*Hollinshed's Chronicles, "Britain,"* 125)

*WHY IS DAN ALONE, OF ALL THE TRIBES OF ISRAEL, OMITTED IN THE SEALING OF THE 144,000? (Rev. 7)

*Paper read at an Anglo-Israel meeting in 1874, and printed in an extended form in the *Hebrew Christian Witness*, July, 1875.

This is a question often asked, and one which, in any history of that Tribe, some effort should be made to answer.

The usual answer of commentators is (see Alford) that Dan was the first to fall into idolatry, and that it would, therefore, be obliterated.

This may be at once disposed of as incorrect by a reference to Ezekiel 48, where, in the division of the land which has never yet taken place, Dan comes in for this share at the head of the list; therefore, at that blessed time, Dan will still be as much in favour with God as any of the other Tribes.

The error possibly has arisen, in some measure, from assuming that the sealing mentioned is to take place at the day of judgment, or at the ushering in of some new dispensation. This view also has been favoured by the picture in the last part of the chapter – viz., the *countless* multitude with palms in their hands, who are generally supposed to represent saved *Gentiles*. Commentators have often satisfied themselves with this interpretation: that the saved *Gentiles* shall be *countless*, but that the saved of faithful Abraham's seed – of him to whom so much was promised – are only to amount to 144,000 – less than an average modern army of a first-class European State, and less than a *quarter* of the number of *fighting men alone* who came out of Egypt under Moses upwards of 3,000 years ago! Why, so long ago as in Elijah's day, God had reserved to Himself in Israel 7,000 men *"who had not bowed the knee to Baal."*

A very brief examination of the vision of the seals (Rev. 5-9) will show (1st) that the sealing took place during an interlude between the sixth and seventh seals; and (2nd) that the object of the sealing was to preserve alive *upon the earth* certain of God's people – Israel – during certain calamities which were about to be brought upon the earth *under the seventh seal.*

Similar instances are the *blood over the door* in Egypt, which secured the inmates against the destroying angel (Exod. 12:23); see a sealing also (Ezek. 9:4-6); see also Rev. 9:4, where in one of the judgments of the seventh seal, and under the fifth trumpet, it is distinctly said that they were *"not to hurt. . . . . but only those men which have not the seal of God in their foreheads."*

It will now be asked, Who, then, are the countless multitude with palms in their hands of ver. 9? To this I conceive the answer to be that it is customary in the Word of God, wherever calamities are foretold (see especially Isaiah), to follow them up with verses or a whole chapter of comfort and blessing; and in the present case, ver. 9 to the end of the chapter is, I think, a glimpse of heaven, depicting, for the comfort and assurance of the Church on earth when trouble and danger threaten, the perfect peace and comfort of those who endure faithfully to the end. Thus the first part of the chapter gives warning of the tribulation impending, and takes precautions for the safety of the elect, and the last part of the chapter holds up to view the reward.

Let us now see if there is anything to show where these 144,000 could have been at the time of the sealing.

To elucidate this, let us examine the sixth chapter, which details the events under the first to the sixth seals.

As each seal was broken, there was exhibited to St. John, as it were, a picture, each of which pictures the apostle describes, recording, at the same time, utterances which sometimes accompanied the exhibition. The six seals are in this way broken in succession, the first of which is considered by many commentators to be an assuring symbol of the progress and triumph of the kingdom of Christ;* the other five being, by the consent of commentators, from whom I see no reason to differ, events *now historical* and well identified – fearful wars, principally affecting Greeks, Romans, and

Jews – scarcity of food – dreadful persecutions and massacres of Christians, including the period known as the era of martyrs (A.D. 270-304), and the last fierce struggle of Paganism against Christianity, which ended in the triumph of Constantine, A.D. 323.

---

*Elliott, however, believes that the *white horse* must be Rome; but, if so, what of Rev. 19:11?

The verses at the close of the sixth chapter, being the end of the *sixth* seal, describing the terror of the followers of Paganism, have led casual readers to suppose that it represents the end of the world – *the last day*; but it is clearly not so. For whatever be the interpretation, there still remains the long string of judgments to be accomplished upon the earth under the *seventh* seal.

Why, then, were these 144,000 of Israel (omitting Dan) to be sealed *now*, *after* the *sixth* seal and just before the seventh? One must infer that the judgments hitherto, which embraced the period called the "Era of Martyrs," and which extended over the whole *Roman* Empire, including Egypt and Syria, had not materially affected them, or surely they would have been sealed at the outset.

If we accept the Scythians and Goths as representing Israel, we get out of this difficulty at once. Between the Danube and the Don *they* had enjoyed for centuries wonderful security. They had spread south of the Danube, and had there, it is true, come into fierce collision with the Romans, sometimes triumphing, sometimes failing, *but the heart of their country had never been penetrated.*

Keatinge, the Irish historian, rejoicing that Ireland was partly peopled by batches of Scythians or Scots from Gothland in the Euxine, says at p. 54:

"Justin, the abbreviator of Trogus, gives this glorious account of the Scythian nation: – 'The Scythians were always free from the attempts of any other nation, or came off conquerors when they were attacked. They drove Darius, the Persian king, out of Scythia, who was glad to save himself by a cowardly and ignominious flight. They killed Cyrus and his whole army. They fought with the same success against Zopyron, one of Alexander's generals, and destroyed him and all his forces. They have heard indeed of the arms of the Romans, but never felt them.' A character that no other people of the world so eminently deserved, and which we have no reason to suspect of partiality, as it came from an author who was a Roman."

Thus then, on the north of the Black Sea, the Goths and Scythians had been entirely out of the way of the judgments under the first six seals. Christianity had taken root among them; there was a Gothic bishop present at the council of Nicea, A.D. 325, Uphilas, who had translated the Lord's prayer and the greater part of the Bible into Moeso Gothic.

What was now to happen that the sealing should take place before the opening of the seventh seal? It is remarkable, and it is strong evidence in favour of the Identity of the Goths or Scythians with Israel, that, by all commentators, the events under the first *trumpet* (*i.e.,* on the opening of the seventh seal) are held to be the *irruption of the Goths upon the Roman Empire*, A.D. 338-412. They had been surging up for some years, and now, pressed upon in the East by the Huns, they burst forth upon the West. As if God, before He put His host, His "sanctified ones" (Isa. 13:3), His special hidden instruments, in motion (*"Thou art My battle axe"*) to execute His purpose, had numbered 144,000 of them to Himself, to preserve a people to Himself, and a seed to Abraham, out of the myriads exposed to peril.

Why then was not Dan sealed?

The calamities against which the sealing was a safeguard, and in which the Goths were the instruments used by the Almighty, were to sweep over the Roman Empire. But if we accept as a fact that Dan, instead of being led away by the Assyrian conquerors and wandering about with the other Tribes, making long land journeys, preferred to take to his ships, abandoning Palestine, Greece, and the Black Sea, as enemies made them too hot and unsafe, and to seek the secure and remote West, destined by God as Israel's sanctuary, then, there is a plain reason why it was *not necessary that this Tribe should be sealed,* for *it was not endangered.* Denmark, Devonshire (Danonnia), Scotland, and Ireland *were not within the theatre of operations.*

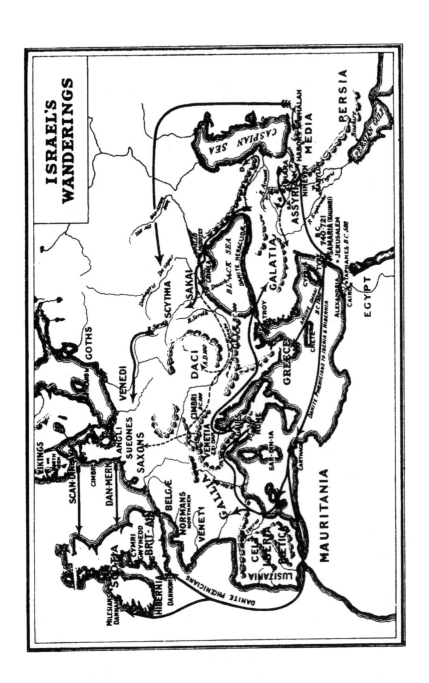

WHAT THE SCYTHIANS SAID TO HERODOTUS
AT THE PORT OF BORYSTHENES

In the preceding pages various points of resemblance between the Scythians and Israelites have been brought forward.

1. The Hebrew etymology of the name *Scythian* (p. 31).

2. Their first mention by profane historians *"of mean original* on the Araxes" (Diodorus ii. 3) accords with the *position* of exiled Israel.

3. The period assigned by Herodotus (i. 15) to disturbances among the peoples of Asia Minor, caused by the movements of the Scythians – viz., in the reign of Ardys, the son of Gyges, circ. 680 to 630 B.C. – allows some fifty years or more from the date of the captivity of Israel, cir. B.C. 740/or 720, within which a people with Israel's blood and training could have rallied and asserted themselves.

4. Their learning (*Herod.* iv. 46).

5. Their excellent laws (*Strabo* viii. iii. 7, and vii. iii. 7).

6. Their prejudice against swine (*Herod.* iv. 63).

7. Specimens of their languages given by Herodotus are Hebrew (p. 35).

8. Their gods seem to be Syro-Phoenician (pp. 35-36, extracts from note Blakesley's *Herodotus*).

9. Greek tradition classes them as Heraclidae and connects them with the Lacedaemonians, whose relationship was acknowledged by the Jews (pp. 19, 31).

10. But what the Scythians themselves told Herodotus is, so far as it is intelligible, just as remarkable. "The Scythians say theirs is the *most recent of all nations.*" (*Herod.* iv. 5) Moses said to Israel: *"The Lord did not set His love upon you because ye were*

more in number than any other people; for ye were the fewest of all people." (Deut. 7:7) Again: *"A Syrian* [Heb. *Arami*] *and ready to perish was my father, and he went down to Egypt, and sojourned there with a few, and became there a nation, great, mighty, and populous."* (Deut. 26:5)

11. "The Scythians say that the first man that appeared in this country,* *which was a wilderness,* was named Targitaus; they reckon the number of years from their first beginning, from King Targitaus to the time that Darius crossed over against them, to be not more than a thousand years, but just that number." (*Herod.* iv., sec. 7)

"This Country." There is nothing opposed to our theory of the Scythians being Israel in Herodotus' account that *the wilderness* they referred to was in *Scythia;* whether they really asserted it themselves, or whether he merely supposed that they spoke of the country they then occupied. In the traditions of the flood, so common among many races throughout the world, some neighbouring high mountain generally does duty for Mount Ararat, and is pointed out as the one on which the people were saved. So also that part of the Scythian tradition which indicates the river *Borysthenes* instead of *the Nile* as the mother of their king.

Darius' expedition against the Scythians took place about B.C. 500, so that 1500 B.C. would be the date of the appearance of their king Targitaus *"in the wilderness."* 1500 B.C. is also about the date of the appearance of Israel under Moses *in the wilderness.* Until then they had been a leaderless community of Egyptian slaves.

These numerous points of resemblance between the Scythians would lead one to expect that, if really Israelites, the curious legend related by them to Herodotus (iv. 5-7) ought to reveal something *specially* Israelitish; though coming to us second hand, through Herodotus, we might naturally expect it to be somewhat blurred and defaced.

I suggest that Herodotus, in writing down the Scythian legend, spelt in Greek characters, as nearly as he thought they pronounced them, the names of certain things mentioned by the Scythians, and that his transcribers, meeting with words which they did not understand, altered the spelling to make them comprehensible Greek words; or else, that Herodotus himself made the blunder, and wrote what he thought they said. I place Herodotus' version side by side with my suggested interpretation of the legend, including the words which I suppose to have been uttered by the Scythians, and stumbled at by Herodotus or his transcribers.

HERODOTUS' VERSION	SUGGESTED INTERPRETATION
1. The first man that appeared in this country, which was a wilderness, was named *Targitaus*.	1. Israel first became a nation in the wilderness under *Thagedoos* אתהעדות (the testimony, covenant).*
2. They say that the parents of this *Targitaus* were *Jupiter* and a *daughter of the river Borysthenes*.	2. Thagedoos (the Testimony) emanated from Jehovah, and was given through one *drawn out of a river* (Moses - Exod. 2:10).
3. That he had *three* sons.	3. The service of the Mishcan-ha-Geduth (Tabernacle of the Testimony) was administered by a family of *three* (Moses, Aaron, Miriam).

---

* אתהעדות , eth-ha-gedoos (plural) the *testimony, covenant,* or *witness, is the general name for the various types and appointments of the law* delivered by God through Moses. There was the מ שׁכן העדת , Mishcan-ha-Geduth, the *dwelling*, or tabernacle, of the *Testimony*, or *witness* (Exod. 38:21; Num. 17:7). The Cherubim with the ark were called העדות (Exod. 30:6). The two tables (לחת) were called העדת , tables of the *Testimony*, or *covenant*, as containing what the Israelites on their part were to do, and not to do. (Exod. 31:18)

ת is pronounced either as *th* or as *s*. In most of the London synagogues it is pronounced *s*. ע *For the G pronunciation see Gesenius.* עזה, *Gaza* (Gen. x, 19), and עמרה. (Gen. xviii. 20), Gomorrah.

---

4. That during their reign, φερομενα χρυσεα ποιηματα *produced of golden workmanship*, (plural, referring to all),

αροτρον , *arotron*, a plough.

ζυγον , *zugon*, a yoke, nom. *zugos*,

σαγαριν , *sagarin*, an axe, and a bowl.

4. The sacred things within the Holy of Holies, [all except the tables being made of *gold*, or *overlaid* with *gold*,] were (Heb. 9:3-5):

Aron, ארון the ark (of the covenant).

Hlukos,* לחת, the tables (of the covenant).

'*S-ha-krvim*, אתהכרבים , the cherubim (Heb. 9:5).

And the *golden pot*‡ (that had the manna) (Heb. 9:4).

5. Dropping down from heaven, fell on the Scythian territory.

5. The tables themselves, and the *patterns* of the rest, were given direct by Jehovah to Moses. (Exod. 25:40, 31:18; Heb. 8:5)

---

* לחת, *hlukos*, tables. The ancient *I*, I think, had the sound of the Welsh *Ll* in Llanberis, Llangollen, which is approximately expressed by *Hl*. This sound often becomes in the mouths of the inexperienced *sh*. In Kaffir there is the same sound, *Hlamba, to wash*, and *Umhle, handsome*, &c., invariably pronounced by inexperienced Europeans *Shlamba* and *Mooshle*. And we have an instance of the Greek becoming *z*, in the little island near Malta, formerly *Gaulos*, now *Gozzo*. Hence I think לחת , *lukhos, the tables*, might easily have been misunderstood for *zugos*, a yoke.

‡ A bowl is a common article; the Scythians probably knew the Greek word φιαλην., or they would have no difficulty in explaining it to Herodotus.

6. That the eldest, seeing them first, approached, intending to take them up; but, as he came near, the gold began to burn. When he had retired, the second went up, and it did the same again. . . . . But when the youngest went up, the third, it became extinguished. . . . . The elder brothers, in consequence of this, giving way, surrendered the whole authority to the youngest.

6. *"Miriam and Aaron* [the two eldest, Exod. 2:4, 7:7] *spake against Moses* [the youngest of the three]. . . . . *and said, Hath the Lord indeed spoken only by Moses? Hath He not also spoken by us? And the Lord heard it. . . . . And the Lord spake suddenly unto Moses, and unto Aaron, and unto Miriam, Come out, ye three, unto the tabernacle of the congregation. . . . . And the Lord came down in the pillar of the cloud, and stood in the door of the tabernacle, and called Aaron and Miriam, and they both came forth.*

And He said, Hear now My words, If there be a prophet among you . . . . My servant Moses is not so . . . . with him will I speak mouth to mouth . . . . not in dark speeches, and the similitude of the Lord shall he behold: wherefore then were ye not afraid to speak against My servant Moses? And the anger of the Lord was kindled against them, and the cloud departed from off the tabernacle; and behold Miriam became leprous, white as snow. (Num. 12)

Thus the youngest of the three was miraculously chosen, and the two elder gave in.

7. This sacred gold the kings watch with the greatest care, and *annually* approach it with magnificent sacrifices to render it propitious.	7. "But into the second." [the Holiest of all, where the ark and the rest of these things were placed] went the *high priest alone, once every year, not without blood."* (Heb. 9:7; Lev. 16:2, 34)

Such, I think, may be the solution of the Scythian legend of their leader and of their sacred things. For, if any one were asked what things a people of Israelitish descent would be likely to have engrafted into their traditions, would he not reply: of course something connected with that wonderful schooling in the wilderness; of course the Tabernacle of the Testimony, over which, in sight of them all, hung, when at rest, a cloud by day and fire by night and which gave the signal, by the raising of the cloud or fire, for the hosts of Israel to move on. (Exod. 40:34-38) – Of course the mysterious symbols that occupied the centre of worship in the Holy of Holies – that ark overlaid with gold, the ark of the covenant of Jehovah, before which the waters of Jordan clave asunder when the feet of its bearers touched the margin; before which the walls of Jericho fell down; which caused a plague to the Philistines when they captured it, and which threw down their god Dagon so that they were glad to send it away; and the untrained cows leaving their calves behind unguided, except by the will of their Creator, brought it safely back to Israel. – Of course those mysterious emblems, *"the cherubim overshadowing the ark,"* made of pure gold, and *"out of the same lump"* as the mercy-seat; and the tables of the testimony kept within the ark, *"written with the finger of God,"* which Moses brought down from the mount after forty days communing face to face with Jehovah, so that when he re-appeared his face reflected the glory he had witnessed; the precepts engraven on which tables were delivered from Sinai by God Himself to the people, mid thunder, lightning, earthquake, and the sound of a trumpet. So terrible was the sight that even Moses said, *"I do exceedingly fear and quake."*

Such are the things, in addition to the origin of their leader, which it might confidently be anticipated would be impressed for many centuries on the traditions of a people of Israelitish descent, and as such I offer a probable solution of Herodotus' version of the Scythian legends.

It was noticed at page 31 that the Lacedaemonians, the acknowledged relatives of the Jews, and, like the Scythians, *Heraclidae*, say that their ancestor Lacedaemon was a son of Jupiter and Taygeta. Taygets, or Taygetus, was the name given to the mountain overlooking their city Sparta. Their legend seems to describe them as the people of Jehovah through (T-ha-Gedoos) the covenant; and it is curious that an early name of their country was AEbal. (Deut. 27:2-4)